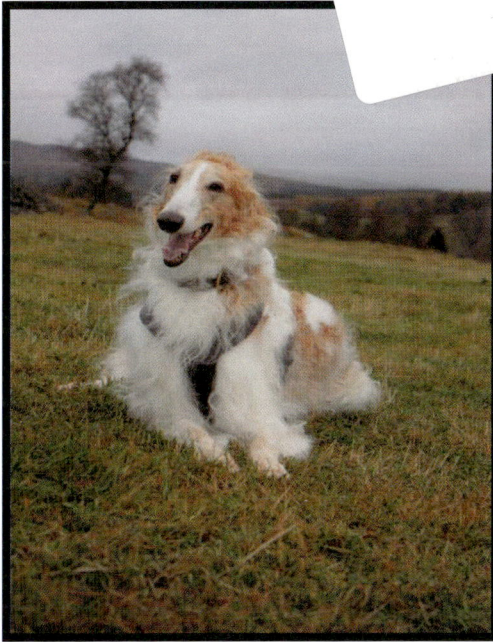

Wish Come True

Gentle ways to help you solve your dogs' behaviour problems.

by Abbie Withers

Copyright © Abbie Withers 2013

Publishing by Wishie Publications, United Kingdom

The information in this book is intended for educational purposes only. It is not intended for diagnosis, prescription or treatment of any health or well-being disorder. The information should not replace consultation with a registered veterinary professional. The author is in no way liable for any misuse of material.

For Wishie my beloved dog and teacher.

About the author

Abbie Withers has always had a strong love and understanding of animals, and since a toddler just seemed to know dogs, their body language and mannerisms.

Not allowed to own one of her own as a child, she went on in later life to own, breed and show several breeds, learning much about behaviour from her own dogs.

Abbie has worked with animals for most of her life as a veterinary nurse and dog groomer and has been fortunate to be involved for several years in the film industry, supplying and training many species for famous tv and photographic productions.

Abbie now works in Scotland helping many people to understand why their dogs are showing behaviour problems, and how to positively solve them using her own method called 'Wish Come True'.

Developed from many years of owning her own very special, at times difficult, Russian Wolfhound Aloysious aka "Wishie", her method helps you positively help your dogs to become calmer, better behaved and altogether happier.

Abbie runs 'The Ark' an exclusive grooming salon in Perth:

THE ARK
for animal wellbeing

Contents

Introduction

A chance encounter with a breeder of Russian Wolfhounds when looking for one to be on set of a BBC period production, led me to fall deeply and utterly in love with the breed and subsequently to owning several of my own.

It was one of these is a dog called Aloysious - Wishie – now almost ten years old – a beautiful, elegant, head strong, free spirited soldier who showed me that trying to restrain and control one so intent on being one body length ahead, no matter what was used or said, was futile. I will always be indebted to him for showing me both in my behaviour and grooming work that if you ask a dog to use his own mind and give him his freedom, he will relax and want to please you more than if tied in chains, held close on a tight lead, abused, reprimanded or punished into submission.

This book is dedicated to and named after my wonderful boy who in his stubbornness has planted the seed of freedom in my mind to be shared with all owners of "unruly" dogs in the world, in the hope that in changing the way you train your dog results in a stronger bond, happier owners and happier dogs.

Thank you Wishie you are my living legacy.

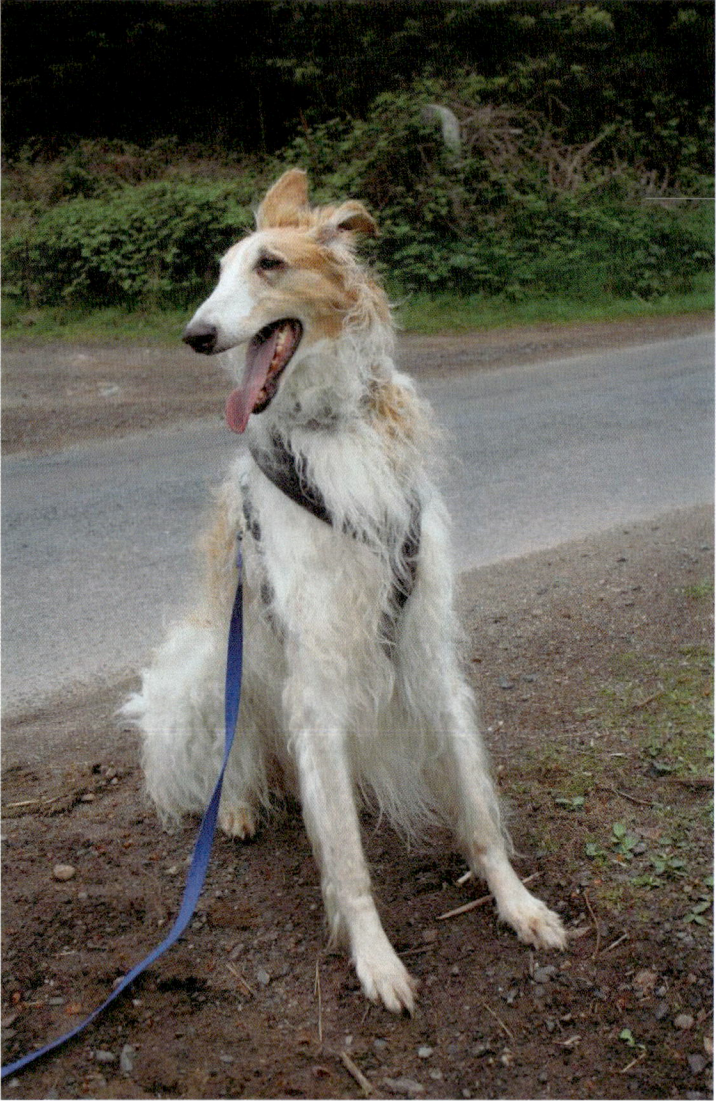

Other training methods

Having been to dog training classes with some of my own dogs over the years, I have come across several other methods of training.

Most I have observed to be organised with large groups of people and their dogs together either in village halls, outbuildings or field situations.

Generally you go along knowing that you need help with your dog, but you feel nervous and unsure of how your dog will react to the new environment, other dogs and their owners. I have heard it said over and over again that people come away feeling useless, intimidated, compared to the rest of the class members and most of all not given enough one to one attention when they need it most, in order to gain their confidence and pass that down to their dogs .

Think of it this way – imagine you are your dog as a young child going to school for the first time: would you prefer to be guided by someone who was afraid/nervous/unsure, or confident and able to teach you calmly, gently and with patience? Who would you learn the most from?

It is important that you become that confident guide and this is what I aim to instil into any dog owner who comes to me for help.

Something I come across often is people being shunned from training classes as their dogs seemed unruly, or people who have given the classes up themselves as perhaps they feel they are not as good as the one person in the class whose dog is behaving perfectly and gets every command first time.

This is why I offer purely one to one consultations, not to make judgements of peoples errors with their dogs but to help them feel great about what they can do for and with their dogs and it is by observing these and showing how important it is to always follow up with immediate praise, in order to help your dog understand right from wrong.

I start within the home with my consultation work, as it is important for people to understand how vital it is that they are showing their dogs consistently where they belong within the family and I inevitably see where things have been going wrong to date and the errors people make by inadvertently sending the wrong information to their dogs in many different ways – most dogs I am asked to go out to help have problems because they have been confused by conflicting signals/commands given by different family members.

I often jokingly say, I am a people whisperer not a dog whisperer, but I know it is more or less true. People think dogs think like people and this is where the birth of the errors lies within communication between the two species.

I begin by meeting all of the members in the family and dogs, and by making observations of how everyone communicates with the dog and how he reacts with everyone in return. How the family communicates can be unintentionally forcing their animal to feel stressed or overburdened with unnecessary tasks or jobs – i.e. to be protector or guard by looking out of a window all day or left to run around a garden all day via a dog flap into the garden – is it any wonder your dog barks at anything and everything that moves in the vicinity as he feels it his duty to protect it and is then confused by being reprimanded for doing so?

If within the home your dog feels he is in charge of the rest of his family it is no wonder that when he is out in the wider world that all sorts of problems arise.

For instance say a young puppy of ten months is allowed to bark non stop at people or cars passing the window or rush to the front door whenever someone knocks or rings the bell with no communication to advise him otherwise, then in his mind he considers it is his duty to be caring for his family at even such an early age. Why then would things suddenly change when you take him outdoors to the park? In fact allowing him to stay at this heightened level of position in the family (pack in his eyes) at such a young age can lead to major problems if not injury from other dogs. He is not yet able to carry such responsibilities and is living his life in a stressed state which can also lead to illnesses – skin or digestive disorders can manifest in some cases due to the stresses which he is may be carrying.

It is important to learn how to help your dog by invisibly demoting him – in other words taking the weight of the world off his shoulders to allow him to relax back into enjoying life without such responsibilities and you will have a much more enjoyable relationship with your dog once again, instead of constantly shouting at/ constantly jerking your dog back to you on a collar and lead /chasing after him when he runs off with no intention of listening to you on a walk.

There is a lot I can help you with within your home environment, by way of making small changes which make a huge difference to your dogs' behaviour when the time comes to go out with him.

I will now cover some of the methods which other trainers may suggest you use and the reasons why I do not approve of them.

Choke Chains, half-choke and prong collars , haltis etc.

These collars are commonly sold and sadly still used in this country. I dislike all of these with a passion because they are negative, forceful devises used by owners who have had no help in understanding the dogs' mind and how to ask of him instead of forcing him to do something against his free will.

Only recently I was asked to go to help a beautiful young male German shepherd whose owner was on the point of considering rehoming him – in her desperation she rang the Dog Borstal programme who suggested they get in touch with me as I was local to her. When I arrived at her home I was given lots of information that previous trainers had passed on to try to help this dog – most of which in my mind were negative methods – tools used to force her dog into submission and something I find incredible to believe was that she was, as a last resort, told to buy a prong collar to use on him so she could actually walk him.

When I see someone using a halti on a dogs face while taking him for a walk I truly feel very sad for the dog. Obviously what has happened is the owner did not enjoy being pulled by his dog while walking him and perhaps could not find anyone who could train him how to help his dog want to be beside him so has resorted to a suggestion that using a restraining tool would make things much better. Better for who? A dog needs to use his nose as he walks along for many reasons which I will mention later in the book but suffice to say while wearing such a devise he has no way of knowing what is in his immediate area in order to protect himself, nor fully enjoy his time outside, as his head is off the ground and he is forced to walk in a straight line beside his owner - which also means he is not getting the exercise or interests that he could be getting while on a harness and longer line.

Understandably a shorter lead is necessary for walking in busier places.

A prong collar is a metal device with short prongs facing into the dogs neck and if the dog pulls the collar tightens and he is given immediate pain. Pain is not conducive to positive learning and positive learning has a much longer lasting benefit to all concerned. I could not imagine anything worse for a dog and wish they were banned from this country – this way of training a dog is not something I condone and is far from the positive methods I use where the dog uses his own mind in a relaxed way with no pain and which can quickly show you how a strong and loving bond is created.

The moment when I see this happening is why I love my work so much – when owner and dog come together willingly, effortlessly and happily is beyond words and very rewarding to both me and the previously stressed out owners. It truly gives me goose bumps.

Once you understand that showing an animal how he can use his own mind to decide if something is acceptable or not instead of being forced into doing something is when your relationship with your dog becomes a whole lot happier and more rewarding in many, many ways.

I work to promote positive behaviour in dogs and show you how to do the same and how by doing so the negative problems begin to fade and are gone permanently.

Shock & Citronella Collars

A shock collar is one which is fitted with a device which either vibrates or sends an electric shock of differing levels, set by the owner, to the neck of the dog. Many people will buy these and without learning how to use them think they are for stopping an animal doing something immediately at the highest shock level.

At whatever level either the vibration or shock setting I consider them to be a negative tool and a cruel and lazy way for humans to make an animal react to an action he or she may be doing as a normal canine behaviour. Dogs do not think like we humans do and do not understand what is being asked of them – they become scared and have not learned what a human is asking of them and this fear can manifest in other ways such as biting - striking out or even in health problems.

I wish they were banned here as they are in Wales.

Citronella collars are similar in they carry a pack of lemon scented gas which sprays the dog in the face if the noise it makes is loud enough – i.e. barking. Unfortunately Citronella is a carcinogen and cancers have been found to appear at the site of the spray

Barking is a dogs own way of communicating and is a complex behaviour interaction. Preventing an animal using its' voice can cause deeper issues by making the animal afraid of using the only method of communication it has.

It is far better to seek help with education of canine behaviour and communication so as to help with you with your dogs' personal issues.

Some common errors in Communication between owners and dogs

a) Feeding

As a provider and guide / protector to your dog, a major factor within a pack – your household - is who provides and feeds food – the supporter of health and life itself.

Many people these days seek the easy route with their dogs and feed processed foods some of which come in dry format which can be left in a dish all day for their animals.

Apart from loathing of feeding processed foods of any kind to animals, something I will cover in another chapter, leaving a bowl of dry food down all day for your dog is something which is giving a signal to your dog that you are not a provider and it is therefore planting a seed in his mind that there is another reason for him to try to be that provider and to raise himself within the pack – your family – another reason which can add to behaviour problems – another stress for your dog.

Food is a vital part of your dogs' life and he deserves to be given real, fresh, species appropriate food from you and for you to be seen to do so.

Feed your dog a nourishing fresh meal twice a day after you have eaten your own meal.

Make sure he sees you prepare his meal and put it down for him in his own dish. If he does not eat it after a few minutes it is important to lift it and offer nothing else until his following meal.

This way you are establishing with him that you are his provider.

There is little bond between a dog and his owner when he is allowed to pick all day from a boring bowl of cardboard artificial tasteless food.

b) How to give your dog a reason to listen to you

If you are experiencing problems with your dog and you most likely are or you would not be reading this book, it doesn't matter what the problem is – i.e. I am often called to help and the owner rattles off a list of issues - it could be one or all of these:

- barking at people or other dogs

- jumping up,

- chasing wheels of cars,

- pulling on the lead,

- destroying belongings or parts of the house itself,

- separation anxiety,

- fear aggression

- fear of fireworks / loud noises.

but most of the problems can be taken back to the fact that the dog does not consider you to be his guide enough to listen to you or trust you and has decided to deal with the world and its' situations by himself. Yet more often than not I see young dogs who are no where near ready to cope with the world out there and all its dangers despite what they think themselves. They need you to be their guide and protector.

If you do not get this right from the time you start your relationship with your dog within your own home environment, which he considers to be his pack, there is no doubt that problems will manifest in one form or another at some point.

It is not difficult to show your dog that you are the one who is responsible to protect him, guide him and provide for him.

It is not necessary in any way to be physically negative to your dog. When you shout at or hit a dog it is adding to his problems and not in any way helping him to understand what you are asking of him.

Shouting at a dog is raising the energy which in turns is sending an exciting energy to him/her or making him very nervous of you indeed. Why would you trust someone who frightens you?

This book is about learning how to help your dog positively which reaps rewards in a calm and enjoyable way, the results from which will begin almost immediately and will remain between you and your dog for the duration of his life if done consistently and by everyone within the home.

If other members of the family and anyone visiting do not use the same methods, then you will no doubt see a re-occurrence of behaviour problems.

c) Attention seeking
Some dogs will try to get your attention at any cost. Barking, running around, bringing you a toy, whining, licking your hand or foot, even scratching themselves, are all ways in which he learns how he gets a reaction.

Staring at you until you look at or touch your dog is something you particularly need to pay attention to. Eye contact is a huge reward and I advise you do not give eye contact when you are being begged into giving it and turn your head away to the side until your dog relaxes.

They are ploys to raise himself in the in his mind – if he instigates play and also ends it he is giving himself permission to be superior. If your dog brings you a toy and you play tug of war with him and let him have it at the end he is now the boss. Little things like this all add up to having an unruly dog in the long term. They may seem a little on the severe side but I know when you make small changes you will reap huge rewards in the long run.

d)   Mixed Messages
If all members of the family, including children, do not use the same commands, signals etc. with their dog then he will be confused as to know what he can or cannot do and behaviour issues begin. Always the opportunist any dog will promote himself as soon as he sees a chink through which to squeeze.

 i.e. a dog who is fed by the father of the family in his own dish and not allowed to scrounge from the dinner table until the teenage daughter feeds him from her plate, causing the dog to sense that he has been promoted - pack leaders do not share food but eat until they have had enough, sending a clear message to others of their position, leaving the remainder to its subordinates is a clear message - mixed messages can make a dog feel confused as to where they are within your family.

e) Separation Anxiety

When leaving your home without your dog there are important things to remember which will help prevent your dog suffering separation anxiety.

This can show itself in many forms from howling or barking, destruction of belongings or furniture – I have seen several dogs destroying door frames, wallpaper and lino – or in some cases even causing dogs to have colitis or skin disorders.

I am often called to houses by people saying their dog howls when they leave without their dog or their neighbours are complaining when people are out at work about the noise of whining or barking dogs and sometimes it can be a very serious situation when the threat of court procedures are mentioned.

What is separation anxiety?

When a dog is given mixed signals by its owners and is unsure where he feels most comfortable and relaxed in his mind he will certainly feel stressed if the members of his pack, who he considers to be below him, suddenly leave without him. The greater the way this stress manifests shows me the enormity of the problem you may have with him.

He is basically trying to cope with a huge concern regarding the members of the family for whom he feels responsible – his job is vast on a daily basis and suddenly everyone leaves – it is too much for him and he will either cry out by barking or howling or in a state of panic begin to tear at his surroundings.

Just one of the door frames ruined by a collie I visited with
separation anxiety.

So, how to help him?

If you have an older dog showing signs of separation anxiety or a
new puppy in your family, it is important to begin by putting a rule
into place that everyone must do each time they leave home or
return.

When leaving do not look at, touch, speak or give anything by way
of a treat to your dog, simply leave. Obviously you will know he is
left in a safe area of your home where he has a comfortable place to
lay and with access to clean water. When starting this technique
begin by going out for only a few minutes –walk round the block,
along the road, or into the garden. Just enough time for your dog to
think you have gone out and will not know when you will return.

Upon your return it is equally important to completely ignore your
dog for a few minutes – five minutes is usually best. The more

anxious the dog the longer it may take for him to settle down again, but you must wait for him to do so before making any contact again.

Do not look at him, speak to him nor touch him and if he jumps up at you turn your back as many times as is necessary for him to stop doing so – and when and only when he is calm, preferably lying down go to him and down at his level and ask him to come to you to speak to him and touch him gently.

By building this up over time from three or four minutes to ten then twenty minute stretches you will see it will become a very effective way to relieve your dog of one of the jobs he feels responsible for which has caused him to be so anxious.

f)   Tug of War

All dogs benefit from exercise and play, and by playing with toys or balls with your dog you can build a bond between you. It is great fun to see your dog so active and able to jump high or run so fast after objects such as Frisbees or tennis balls thrown from long handled ball throwers, so long as the game is instigated from you and finished by you.

Tug toys are really popular and long lasting toys for dogs, commonly bought for puppies as they are chewable and gentle on their soft mouths, but always make sure you are the one ending the tug of war game and do not let your dog have the toy last, as this is another self promotion for your dog in his way of thinking.

If he instigates play by bringing a toy to you it is best to walk away or turn your back – only do so when you initiate and preferably from when your dog is in a calm state.

g)   Fear of fireworks

Many animals are afraid of fireworks but as dogs in the main live in our homes with us and can be very afraid when they hear the loud screams and bangs that fireworks make. We see their reactions and want to make them feel better in the only way we know how as human beings and that is reassurance, either verbally or by touching or cuddling them.

Because by doing so a dog feels reassured that it is alright to remain afraid he will continue to feel so.

A bandage wrap around the shoulders and across the chest will reassure a frightened dog yet without human emotional attachment and will feel gentle pressure which will calm him down.

Further information can be found here:

http://www.tilleyfarm.co.uk/TTouch1.shtml

A Thundershirt, is a great product which works on the same basis as a bandage wrap, supporting the dog without emotional attachment from its owner .They are manufactured in several different sizes to fit most breeds. I have found them to be beneficial to many dogs and not only for fear of fireworks but also change of environment, refusing to eat, stressed and panting while going out in the car, rescue dogs who show signs of not liking either gender of humans.

I suggest trying a Thundershirt for many behaviour issues especially for fear aggression and fear of noises.

I supply and sell a lot around firework night and New Years Eve. They can also be obtained from pet shops across the country.

Using treats as a reward and the options of looking, talking and touching

Most people nowadays feel obliged to give their dog food treats as a reward for behaviour – some give them to their dogs when they have to leave them. This is a human emotion – guilt – something to make us feel better about leaving because we as a human would not like it.

It is big business manufacturing processed treats for dogs and cats. I personally do not like these and never use them with my own dogs, as I do not like the ingredients, Most of them and are highly coloured and preserved with chemicals which I feel unsafe and they can add to behaviour issues and dietary problems. If I ever use food treats I make my own so I know what is in them – liver cake is the most favourite with my dogs and is not difficult to make.

So here is how to make liver cake:

250 g liver (use new Zealand lamb where possible as they use less chemicals in farming) 125 g self-raising flour, 2 eggs, 2 cloves of garlic.

1. Chop the liver into small pieces.
2. Mash the liver in a food processor
3. Add the flour, eggs and garlic.
4. Mix everything together.
5. Place mixture in a greased tray or cake tin.
6. Bake in the oven at 180 degrees C (gas mark 4) for approximately 30 minutes.
7. When ready, remove from the oven and leave to cool.
8. Then simply cut the cake into small squares, split into bags and place in the freezer for future use.

Most people feel a food treat is the only way we can show our dogs how much we appreciate them or reward them for their good behaviour, but did you realise how many other ways we can do so? A touch, a verbal praise and eye contact,   yes eye contact is as big a reward to dogs as anything we feed them.

Eye contact between a group of dogs is a major language and a status symbol, a sign of respect and only given from one to another when that is gained and honoured. We as humans give eye contact all too willingly to our dogs and by doing so too often can again be sending confusing signals therefore unwittingly causing behaviour issues.

Eye contact is something which is a signal of respect between you and your dog and needs to be earned. Some people will tell me their dog sits at their feet in the lounge staring at them as a way in for attention, once contact is given the dog invites himself in to your space and inevitably up onto your knee – who is calling the shots when that happens?

It is a small signal but can make a huge difference to how your dog behaves and something I find most owners do not realise. If you do not want to give your dog permission to be pushy in whatever way try lessening the eye contact you have with him.

It is also interesting to try realising how you are using your voice in the way you praise your dog.

I observe people when they want their dogs to come back to them after they have had time off the lead. If the dog does not respond or runs the opposite way I so often hear people shouting louder and angrier at their dogs. Would you run back willingly to someone who was shouting angrily at you? I know how distressing it can be as well as frustrating when your dog runs off, but try to make it fun, even exciting, give them a reason why being beside you is the best place in the whole world to be. Raise the tone in your voice, use a whistle as an option to get his attention or a hidden squeaky toy and when you have it turn your back and run in the opposite direction. I find this is irresistible to most dogs and when they come running praise them so much they think it's Christmas by way of you either feeding their most favourite treat (home made preferably) or excited praise of "Good Boy/ Good Girl" and a chest rub or a play with a favourite toy. He has done great and you need to make sure he knows it.

This is recall training and you need to repeat it regularly to gain the benefits.

Sometimes I am asked to help because their dog will come back to them, but as soon as they try to put the lead on their collar the dog darts away.

When training a puppy to come back to you a good tip is to touch his collar and highly praise him each time he comes over to you at home and in the garden.

This can help avoid a dog pre-empting you when you are out by only coming so far back to you to avoid having his lead put back on.

You can use this method with older dogs to, by doing it at home before feeding and from time to time by calling your dog to you and touching his collar for a moment before stroking and praising him. It can help to desensitise him to something he does not like.

Punishment – why it doesn't work

Physical or verbal punishment is something which we as humans know as a very clear message from another to stop doing something and as we wish to avoid pain we usually learn to avoid the consequences at all cost.

When it comes to dogs their thought processes are very different than humans. It may make an owner satisfied emotionally that his dog has been taught a lesson once and for all by smacking him but all a dog knows is a loud tone of voice and or pain, not that he must not do that again or else there will be negative consequences.

More often than not a dog may be physically reprimanded well after an event has taken place i.e. an owner coming home to find a chewed shoe or upturned dustbin. If you do not actually find a dog at the time he/she is doing an unwanted behaviour it is entirely unfair to scold him or worse. All your punishments would do to the dog would make him / her very nervous and unsure of you with no connection as to why you are reacting that way and this will affect his future relationship with you. A frightened dog is not a happy dog and one which will find it very difficult to learn from you in the future as you are sending him mixed messages.

If you, as your dogs protector/provider/guide, are not consistent in your manner then your dog will surmise you are failing in some way and once again there is a chink through which he will see a way to show signs of behaviour problems.

Other peoples' dogs etc.

I am often hearing about peoples situations while walking their dog in a public place, where other people and their dogs are. Whether on or off leads I hear some horrendous stories about either their own or others dogs barking, running up to your dog which is on a lead and making you feel very afraid indeed.

At times this has also been another reason why people have given up walking their dogs. Some do not have their own transport to take their dogs somewhere quiet, so a local park is all they have to exercise their dogs in.

If you are unsure as to your dogs behaviour with other dogs or of other peoples dogs approaching then it is important to be sure of your dogs recall and to put in training so as you can be one step ahead of a dangerous situation occurring.

My "Wish Come True" training method was put together for just such owners who lack in confidence as to how to help their dogs return to them when called to get them away from danger.

It is perfectly acceptable when you are walking your dog and do not want other dogs to approach you to shout out at the top of your voice to "Stay Away!!"

I have pre-empted many a potential dog fight by doing this square on to an approaching dog and stamping my foot hard to the ground. It means business and usually makes the dog turn tail.

Another signal for other dog owners to realise you do not want their dog near you is to tie a yellow ribbon midway down onto your lead. This is increasingly being recognised as a nationwide signal to steer clear.

You must also realise that as you have been unsure as to how to help balance your dogs' behaviour that many others out in public also have been and are still.

I have covered how being in a negative or fearful frame of mind effects your dogs' behaviour while out walking, so someone approaching you with their dog could be sending those signals to their own dog which can be a recipe for disaster if the dogs meet head on.

It is very common for people who are unsure of their dogs' behaviour, to pull their dogs tightly on a short lead as soon as they see another dog.

What will this be saying to their already confused animal?

It will be sending a clear signal that another dog is a danger, and their dog who is already considering itself to be in the position to protect and guide its' owner so will be excited to sort the situation in the only way it knows – to lunge and possibly to attack.

Always be on the look out for your dog and do not assume that everyone knows what you now know about how to help him. From now on and especially while you begin your training you need to be his eyes.

Feeding a species appropriate diet

Dogs are carnivores. Not omnivores.

By their very dentition you can tell what food is best for an animals' health, vitality and wellbeing.

Dogs have teeth which are adapted for ripping, tearing and swallowing raw meat and for gnawing at raw bones.

It is true dogs will eat most foods willingly but that does not mean they are doing it any good, in fact may be harming him in some way, either to his health or behaviour.

Processed foods contain hidden ingredients used to bulk out the more expensive ingredients needed by dogs i.e. protein.

Dry foods are made up of a small amount of protein in a large percentage of carbohydrates. Dogs cannot digest carbohydrates very well as they lack the appropriate amount of digestive enzymes to break them down. They cannot utilise all of the food they are given and this results in a sluggish digestion and large amounts of residue resulting in larger, smellier stools.

On a raw diet, more of the food can be digested, therefore more is utilised and there is much less waste. It is advisable not to feed raw meats with processed foods, as they are digested at differing rates and this can cause discomfort to your dog.

Additives, flavourings and colourings in processed foods can cause adverse reactions in our canine friends and are mostly never blamed when side effects occur. Some of these artificial ingredients can be carcinogenic, yet are still used in a lot of dry foods to preserve an open bag for as long as two years. Would you eat something which promised to be the same a year or two down the line as when you opened the bag? The answer to this is a huge no from me.

Dogs deserve real, fresh, species appropriate food at every meal.

A mealtime to a dog ought to be the highlight of his day, next to exercise, something to savour, nourish and satisfy him. When feeding him appropriately his cells will be optimally replaced to build a healthy, strong and vibrant body and his digestive system will work at the rate at which it was designed – quickly and with very strong stomach acids to digest and break down bone and fend off any concerns that we as humans may have of any bugs such as salmonella.

Many people are concerned as to the risk of hygiene when feeding a raw diet, but are unaware that salmonella can be anywhere from supermarket trolleys to a shop door handle.

It is merely a case of using common sense and being hygienic with utensils and dishes, washing your hands after feeding so as to prevent any risk in your home, as you would when preparing your own foods.

I feed a large variety of raw meats to my dogs including green tripe, lamb, chicken, turkey, venison, beef, rabbit, raw eggs, fish, offal and raw meaty bones. I also sell frozen raw meats to my clients in my shop.

For further information regarding raw feeding I have added a link at the end of this book.

The Wish Come True Method

Over the years I have owned many dogs the first of which was a lovely black collie cross Labrador called Poppy. I bought her at the age of 17 years when I left home. Growing up I was not allowed to have any animals of my own and I yearned their company so much so that I spent my free time and holidays walking neighbours' terriers just to be with canines.

Poppy was a very lovely dog, biddable and affectionate and trustworthy. I would walk her in a local park in the city where I lived and she had loads of exercise, always off lead. I began to notice most other dogs were always on a lead and many times owners would ask me what my secret was.

My secret? All I could answer was that your relationship with your dog is based on trust. In order to get it from your dog, you have to give it and reward it and build it up.

To this day I remember the look of amazement on a ladies face when I said if you do not give trust you cannot expect it in return. Quite clever for a seventeen year old I now think.

I trusted Poppy implicitly from the beginning, I gave her what she needed in way of food and love and she gave me back her trust and we had a wonderful bond.

Working with dogs and their owners every day now I hear so many people saying they will never let their puppies or dogs off the lead to run free because they fear they will not come back.

This makes me feel very sad indeed for the dogs. Dogs are born to run.

Fear of dogs running away is a major problem with owners, some have never let their dogs run free since a puppy, others have been kept on a short lead since following an incident i.e. a dog disappearing from view, running over a busy road, being chased by another dog or chasing another dog or wild animal. There is nothing more worrying than knowing you now are not in control of your beloved dog and knowing he would rather be having lots of fun wherever he is than coming running back to you at the first call or worse still perhaps being in danger.

But if you are one of those fearful people unless someone shows you how to train your dog positively, how can you begin to help your dog?

How can you build up the trust?

If you have tried dog training classes without success where do you turn?

I have put together a realistic method which everyone can use with their dogs and at the same time the dog is getting so much more exercise than he ever could have at the end of a short lead while being walked around a park or along a few streets – I have not as yet met anyone who could give a dog as much exercise as it needs while it is still on a lead.

Giving your dog the exercise he needs is allowing him to become a happy balanced one, one with less behaviour issues, one which is much more trainable and a pleasure to have around, a joy to watch.

I begin by telling my own story with my Russian wolfhound.

When I first had him and his brother together they would gambol over the fields and hills and they'd be biddable, returning when called, but as time went on they became a pack and would start to hike it together as soon as my back was turned and there was no getting them back, at times it would be four hours before they re-appeared at my gate, filthy or wet and exhausted with tails a-wagging.

Things became so bad that going out for walks was unbearable and even separately I risked losing one of my beautiful hounds for ever.

A large dog of their size would be shot on site I am sure if they were seen running free over fields whether with or without livestock, so I could not risk this happening. They were not killer dogs in any way but I simply could not afford now to take any risks by letting them run free.

Walking him separately, on a collar and lead he would almost pull my arm out of its socket on occasion and I was at my wits end as to what to do with him.

I took to using long lines on their collars with individual dogs but the pulling was too much to bear especially when the line reached its end. I would even have webbing burns on my fingers from forgetting to release more line. Walking was not fun at all and it soon almost ground to a halt. I was really upset and felt I was a bad owner not being able to exercise her own dogs.

A few years later and Wishie at the age of seven had to be x-rayed around the head and neck areas due to what turned out to be an inner ear infection. It saddened me to be told that he had arthritis all round his right shoulder area.

I had been using a large metal gadget which was sold for using with dogs that pull to take the jolt out of pull, a large spring like on a car suspension, it attached to the collar and then you attached the lead to it. It helped me a little but at the same time had been knocking against him all the while, especially when I pulled him back. I had unwittingly caused him a great deal of injury, which he will feel for the rest of his life.

When he came back form the vets I decided that it was time for a rethink – I researched a comfortable harness to take away from any pressure around his neck and I made him a twenty foot webbing lead with a good strong clip and a padded fleece handle.

I could simply not believe my eyes the first time we went out. For the very first time in all his life on a walk he was free to run where he wanted yet I knew he would not be able to run away for the four hours he had previously loved to do.

He was instantly biddable, where as before he had "selective hearing" and we actually had a fun and relaxed walk together. I still feel guilty for the years I kept this beautiful dog under my confining methods and now know he had a very restricted time while out walking.

Now though, he could use his canine senses (his nose) as he walked along without me feeling his every pull or turn of his neck. Now he could feel confident within himself as he could tell who was in his environment while walking along sniffing verges and walls, plants and kerbs. Was it an entire male or a young female who had previously marked the grass – was he safe or was there a threat ahead or in the neighbourhood?

All of these things are vital to a canine to enable them to balance themselves while out and about. You will begin now to realise what a dog being walked on a collar and lead is missing out on. We as humans can actually be causing problems in terms of behaviour issues, not to mention the damage that pressure from a lead and collar can cause, including eye issues and hypothyroidism. Dogs need to be able to run free – they are born to run.

Hence the "Wish Come True" training method was born and it is what I use to help many a dog who has never been allowed to run free.

To see a dog run at the end of a long line for the first time in a long time is exhilarating to both me and its' owners and I have seen many and shared many a tear of joy with people who have been kind enough to ask of my help.

I am often asked "Do I have to use this long lead forever with my dog?"

The "Wish Come True" training method is the beginning of giving freedom for your dog, which he or she may have never experienced before or you may be using it because your dog has refused to come back to you, and a method in which to build up the response from him/her using positive praise.

Over time of course you can use other leads but only begin when you can honestly answer yourself as feeling confident in your own mind, that your dog is going to come back to you when you called him because you know he wants to. That is how you judge when the timing is right to let him off lead.

Do not ever think that your dog does not know what you are feeling because you will be wrong and I have proven it over and over again.

A positive thinking owner will be walking a happy balanced dog. A nervous or worried owners' dog will misbehave.

Whichever your reason for coming to me for help is it is a method I have put into place to help you build up your confidence with your dog safe in the knowledge that he or she cannot run away, yet is having a good amount of free exercise and being trained in a positive way to come back to you when called.

Work does need putting in between you and your dog while using the long line in order to help your dog realise that being beside you is the best happiest place to be no matter what else may be distracting him so highly positive training by way of the best treats you can bring along and the most exciting praise when your dog comes back to you is of the utmost importance. This needs to be repeated at short regular bursts of ten minutes a day to instil positive results.

It is not a quick fix method by any means and needs to be practised over and over again but as soon as you begin to use it you will see a remarked difference in your dogs' behaviour, which in turn makes walking him a much more positive experience for both of you.

I begin by fitting a comfortable harness on your dog, I use dog – games harnesses (website is at back of this book) as they are well made, well designed, made to measure and very comfortable for your dog, not to mention they come in gorgeous colours too. Then using a twenty foot webbing line I go out with my clients to as big an open space as we can find, preferably somewhere quiet and away from other dogs. If the dog has problems with other dogs I offer a slightly different session initially on a one to one basis, building up such introductions over time.

Dog Games Perfect Fit Harnesses come in all sizes and colours.

Once we are in a large space I ask the owner to just let the dog have a free run using all the length of the line. (if this is the first time he has ever had such freedom it may be only fair to let him experience his freedom for a while and let him run off some excess energy) but keeping hold of the handle end around the right wrist and using the left hand as a guide. Let your dog have fun and encourage him/her to run with you and keep a close eye on him and when you see him run away with his back to you call him with a high voice or use a squeaky toy (previously hidden) and the second you can see him turn his head in your direction, turn around and run in the opposite direction. He will come running and when you can see him out the corner of your eye almost with you, turn round and with open arms highly praise him like you have never done before.

That is it – you have done it!

That is all recall is – a willingness for your dog to do as he is asked i.e. to come straight back to you – no pulling, no jerking just a bond – a very special bond which is so exciting to see and to feel for the first time especially if this is you and your previously "deaf" dog.

If the dog is getting to the end of the line I add in a command such as "steady" or "woah" which over time lets the dog know to slow down so as both of you do not to feel a sudden jerk.

I adore being with a client when their dog willingly comes running back to them when I am out training with them and the more the dog does so the more confident the owner becomes and gradually forgets how awful things previously were when all they saw was the back end of their dog disappearing over that hill.

Confidence is not something that can be bought and so building the confidence up with my clients is my favourite lesson. Once regained I find it does not disappear again and goes a long, long way to mend many behaviour issues that I was asked to help in the first place.

There are many pictures in this book of previously fearful owners who now have gained such confidence through my easy and very rewarding method. I am hopeful that there will be many more too who will ask of my help and through using it there will be so many more happy balanced dogs.

Buster, Tom & his wife Izzy.

Case studies

Buster

Buster was a four month old Bichon puppy when I first met him and his owners. He was brought into my grooming salon to be given his first puppy trim and I distinctly remember chatting to his owners about his behaviour and hearing regarding his processed diet. Buster was proving to be a bit of a handful and already his owners were wondering how they could help him to calm down. Over the next few months he was brought in to be washed / trimmed several times and each time his owner Tom would ask my advice in particular about his running off on walks. Eventually I could tell by the look on Toms face that they needed my help in more ways than one.

The day came for me to go to their home and I picked up on several small things Tom and his wife were doing which gave Buster permission to be in charge of them and their home and I informed them of how to make the changes that would help him calm down. With so many responsibilities Buster was a busy, happy but stressed little fellow.

After an hour or so it was time for me to see him out on a walk and to see for myself what problems Buster had. I was told he was selectively deaf and at times would not return when called and Tom was beside himself with worry.

Fitting a comfy harness and using a 20ft long line we set off on a walk. Initially keeping Buster on a short line Tom felt a marked difference using the harness while we walked around the village.

Buster calmly walking past distractions which previously concerned him.

He was not pulling like he had done previously. When we reached a large open space I asked Tom to let Buster run as free as he wanted at the end of the twenty foot line and to make it fun for him by calling him while running in the opposite direction. Buster complied by running straight after Tom instead of away as before and was treated with mega praise and treats each time he did so.

Buster on a loose line charging back to Tom of his own free will.

When we reached a fully enclosed area I suggested to Tom he let Buster off. I was met with a shocked and worried look but all the same Tom let his little dog go and immediately ran in the opposite direction. Buster ran like the wind to be back with Tom and I doubt I will ever forget the joy on Toms' face and the disbelief at what had just happened.

Walking home was a joy for Tom with Buster closely at heal and glancing upward at his owner from time to time.

Buster off lead showing where he wants to be.

I think the photographs of Busters' consultation speak loudly of giving trust to get it back from your dog. There is nothing like raising a worried owners' confidence by working with them on a one to one basis to share with them the change in their dogs' behaviour – to me it is priceless.

Angel my Staffordshire Bull Terrier saved from death row.

Angel

Two years ago I was approached to help a dog rescue by offering a home to one of their Staffordshire bull terriers on death row. I have a deep soft spot for this fabulous breed as I once bought wonderful female staffie puppy who I called Drostdy and we shared a wonderful 15 years together.

Staffies are a wonderful gentle minded breed with a great sense of humour and need for exercise and fun, they can be very sensitive and demanding yet they are given such bad press. They are not born aggressive with a lust to attack and kill as is commonly and very sadly thought.

However, like a lot of other breeds, if in the wrong hands and treated badly they will react negatively and are much misunderstood.

There was not much history attached to Angel. Suffice to say she had been in a kill shelter and was rescued and placed with a foster carer.

Things sadly began to go wrong and I was asked to advise the lady regarding her behaviour. I was alarmed to hear that she was having great difficulty walking her due to her pulling and she was also trying to attack other dogs. She was being fed hamburgers.

I offered as much advice for free as I would give any client who asks my help, as I truly care when people cannot cope with their dogs. Angel was in London and I could not easily get down to offer a personal consultation.

The last straw came when I had a frantic call. Angel had jumped out of a first floor window to run after and attack a German Shepherd.

The fosterer could no longer cope and asked me if I would I be able to take her in to assess her and help her?

Being over five hundred miles north it was not easy to get her to me, but transport was arranged and I met angel from the train one late summers evening.

She appeared to me to be unfazed by neither the lengthy journey nor her new surroundings but later that evening something was about to happen that shocked even me.

She had at some stage to meet my dogs but careful as I was, she suddenly with absolutely no warning, no change of body language she lunged at one and hung on like a limpet.

I realised very quickly that this girl needed to be treated with kid gloves and very gently re-introduced to a loving home with good food and exercise.

She was really biddable and always came back to me when I called her – she was eager to please and so funny to watch running around on the heather clad hills where I lived. At last she was free and able to get any stresses out of her system.

The months passed and she settled down incredibly well and I eventually began to let her be out with first one dog then two until I could see her body language was not showing signs of threat or fear. All was going very well, she was eating well and enjoying a balanced raw food diet and fitting in nicely in my loving home.

Her favourite food appeared to be raw sardines which she would gulp down head first as though she were a seal. It was too funny.

Then all of a sudden one morning and with absolutely no warning she attacked one of my dogs again. Luckily there was no physical damage done and I managed to separate her but knew deep down that something must be wrong somewhere. I did not know quite what, but I started again with her at the bottom of the heap so to speak and took no precautions with her being alone with my other dogs.

Then I noticed she started to lose some hair. Initially it was a patch on one side at her rear end. She was not itchy in any way and she had no rash. In a short space of time she lost more hair, this time in exactly the same area on the opposite side of her body.

She gradually lost more and more hair and I began to research what may be a reason and while reading an article by Dr. Jean Dodds I realised immediately that she was suffering from a thyroid imbalance.

I took her to the vet, who was not particularly impressed when I refused chemical treatment for parasites. I knew that a thyroid imbalance was a compromised immune system and that by adding chemicals to her already low system that it would cause her more harm. I had eliminated any chance of parasites using the natural methods I use for all of my animals and stood strongly by why I had brought her in to be seen. I wanted a full blood test to check the thyroid levels.

I was correct.

Angel had been quite possibly suffering from a thyroid imbalance for years without anyone checking it out.

If you ask any human who has thyroid problems and they will tell you how constantly tired and grumpy they can feel. They also can lose their hair.

I cannot begin to think how many dogs may be suffering in silence and even put to sleep due to their sudden outbursts of aggressive behaviour.

Angel is on one tablet per day to stabilise her thyroid levels and her blood is checked every six months or so and this is all that is needed for her to be a well balanced and completely happy dog. I have not heard her even so much as grumble at any of my dogs since being on her tablets.

I have never before heard of a dog jumping out of an upstairs window to get to another animal, but she must have been feeling pretty awful to do so.

I am so glad I found out first hand how badly a thyroid problem can affect a dogs' behaviour and I am sure Angel came to me in order that I may make other owners aware that if they have a problematic dog it is advisable to have a simple blood test done in order to check thyroid levels are as they should be.

Dogs cannot speak out when they feel ill and we need to be their voice sometimes.

Thank you Angel for you truly are one.

Samson

Samson

I had a call one afternoon on my mobile from a very friendly gentleman owner of a big, strong, German Shepherd Dog, who explained that he and his wife owned a dog which came from working stock and now he was three years old they were becoming aware that he was too much for them to handle while out on walks. He explained that they had been to training classes with him and he used to be good with other dogs but recently things had changed and walking him, where other dogs might be, was a nightmare for them as he would lunge at other dogs with little warning.

To date they had little success with the previous help they had sought so in desperation they had contacted the Dog Borstal programme in order to try to sort things out.

Because of the distance it was not possible for them to offer help but they passed on my details and I made arrangements to go along for a visit.

I was met by a very exuberant and very beautiful bouncy boy and could immediately see that a lack of stimulation and exercise were a major part of what this boy was missing and needing desperately in order to use up his energy and to stimulate his very intelligent mind.

After an hour or so going over the suggestions of how to help him within the home and his diet etc. we took him out using a long line and watched him enjoy his freedom while his lady owner could see him behaving really well in coming back when called willingly.

It was such a thrill for me to share a once fearful ladies confidence growing with every step and I left knowing that this dog had been given a great chance to show his owners he was not intentionally misbehaving – I had left behind the tools with which to truly help him and give him what he needed.

I visited again a month or so later as I was asked to help in areas where there were more dogs so as to reassure the owner that yes she could be in control of him using a harness with a D ring on the front as well as the top so as to use two leads giving better control.

We took him out to a very busy park on a sunny afternoon and began using my loose lead, high praise positive training method and then with both Samson and his owners we walked with care where other dogs appeared.

On previous occasions Samson would react immediately he saw another dog by tightening his muscles, making himself look bigger and preparing to lunge. As soon as I noticed him start this I suggested to his owner to be one step ahead of him and gently using her body begin to take Samson either confidently past or slightly away from what he considered to be a danger in his mind. As soon as he became calmer, which was immediate, while still walking along to give huge praise and treat him with a tasty treat. Repeating this over and over again his owner became so confident that she could now control his outbursts before they occurred and it was not long before she actually was looking for dogs to walk towards or along side on her own.

Trudie confidently decided to lead Samson closer to other dogs after less than an hour of beginning training knowing she was now a confident owner in full control of her wonderful boy.

I was so taken with her change of frame of mind which was the very reason for her dog being apprehensive in the first place – there was absolutely no stopping her. I left for home knowing that was one lucky dog whose owner now was actually now excited, not afraid to be walking her lovely dog now safe in the knowledge that she had all the tools to help him.

I since have had wonderful updates telling me that he no longer is that lunging dog but " A joy to walk" which is music to my ears.

When you know your dog can be unsafe or nervous around other dogs I suggest you use a yellow ribbon tied to his lead as a sign to other owners to keep their dogs away from yours and do not be afraid to ask others to keep their dogs back – better this way than fretting over injured dogs and angry owners.

A free yellow ribbon can be obtained from: www.yellodoguk.co.uk

Chocolate Labrador Puppy

I was called to a house a few years ago to help a chocolate Labrador pup of nine months.

The lady owner started to rattle off a list of problems – sounding almost proud of his history of mass destruction to date.

I simply said not to worry I do not need to know them all initially because no matter what the problems are they arise from within the home environment and therefore it is where I begin if she was interested in making a booking.

So, along I went with an open mind as I do with all new clients.

I could not have prepared myself for what met me at the door – an absolute whirlwind of bouncing overweight over excited bundle of muscle on legs. I was almost knocked over by his excited energy which up to now had been welcomed and given fuel by every member of the family, looking down at him and touching him and shouting at him to ger-off ger-off!! In a dogs' mind it's all a reward and a reason to carry on and bounce higher and longer until he gets what he wants – ALL the attention – yes it works that does – I'm now the BOSS.

The chaos continued as I walked into one of the hugest kitchens I have ever seen, he managed to rip his claws all down my back in an attempt to get my attention when I turned my back on him – something no one had ever previously done to him. It was as though he had to try anything and everything he could think of as quickly as he could to get a reaction from me so he wiggled all round me as I turned round and walked away, he licked my hands if they were by my side, he actually threw himself onto the two leather armchairs knocking them over in turn in his efforts to get me to look at him but

I was having none of it. It took over half an hour for him to think his efforts were futile and he calmed down slightly for long enough for me to explain my reasons for doing what I had done.

I was met with utter amazement. Never in all the time they had him since a tiny pup had he ever stopped causing chaos, never relaxed, lain down for any length of time and the whole family was at its wits end.

I was met with "how did you do that? What is your secret?"

I explained I had actually relieved him of the job he thought was his since arriving with his new family, that up to now the poor dog has not had a chance to relax without being stressed and was assured that every family member from now on, including visitors, would do what I had done each and every time they came in the house.

For a dog to take half an hour to calm down when someone enters the house tells me the size of the problem with the dog, the actual amount of stress the dog feels he is under.

I suggested he was taken off the processed dry food as soon as possible and started on a species appropriate raw diet as well, so as to eliminate excess colours, additives and preservatives in his system which only add to hyperactivity in dogs.

The chocolate lab was a changed dog from that day forward.

Jills' Mum with Carey (left) and Doug

Carey and Doug.

"Abbie do you think it may be possible to come and help my Mum with her dogs? She is so concerned by one in particular and knows she needs help but she is worried that you will say he needs to be put to sleep." said Jill.

Oh dear, this is the depth of fear that people get to when not knowing how they can sort out negative behaviours with their precious dogs. At times the things that they have in place at home are actually having a reverse effect yet people have no idea until they are made aware.

I was asked to do a house visit to help with a six year old Jack Russell showing aggression when he was asked to do something that he decided he would rather not do.

By aggression I mean growling but also biting, quite severely biting his owner.

I was given minimal information other than the biting and not eating most days and a fearful and little sceptical owner.

I arrived to a lovely house with two barking and jumpy dogs meeting me at the door and when I walked in and ignored them I noticed one run off to grab the nearest toy which he brought to me in the hope it would get my attention.

I was led outside onto a large patio where Jill and her Mum sat with me while I began to get to the bottom of things.

Jills' Mum listened a while to me but soon began questioning with lots of "buts" and "whys". I do like when this happens as it brings out more reasons as to why there are so many problems but I did begin to feel I was hitting a bit of a brick wall until suddenly tears started to fall.

I cannot always assume that everyone feels the same way about asking for help. Some accept suggestions willingly but it was clear that something deeper was going on and it did take quite a while for it to become clear.

Jills' mum had been so worried about her misbehaving dogs but inside was totally blaming herself, feeling guilty but mostly was really worried that if she made changes that would it upset the dogs and her relationship with them would never be the same. She had had several dogs before and none had proven so difficult and she felt so awful at not being able to sort it out.

I really felt for her and reassured her that this would not happen but I would have to finish sharing important information in order to help her put things in place.

I noticed her two dogs were constantly running around the perimeter of the garden looking for anything that moved or made a noise, always jumping up on their owners' knee and bringing toys. There was not much relaxing going on and I knew that Carey in particular was carrying a big burden of being all things to his owner but that Doug was also lying up high on a garden seat above everyone. There was a battle of supremacy going on and as I was walked around the house more became clear. In the large lounge I saw two small dog crates with comfy cushions on the top placed at the low windows which looked over the road. This was a perfect place for little Jack Russell's to lie throughout the day and keep watch and bark if anything became a threat, i.e. neighbours, children, postmen etc.

I was given a tour of the house and found n the main bedroom there were another two crates one placed on top of another for space reasons. When asking who went in each crate I was told Carey goes in the bottom and Doug who was two years old goes in the one on top.

Interestingly, Doug had been promoted over Carey whether he liked it or not causing the mixed messages to add to Careys' confusion.

When it came to feeding Carey would not always eat his food and at times he would not eat at all. Food was not exciting to him yet he was on the grumpy side which manifested when he was asked to do anything, most of all while being put into the back of the car when he quite viciously bit his owner in revolt.

When I was told he was on dry processed food I explained how awful I consider it to be for dogs (for all animals) and how much better a canine appropriate diet of raw meat and bone would be for him. Real fresh nutrients in his system daily would go a long way to balance him and help him. I was met with a little doubt but the seed was planted and we moved on to witness exactly what did happen when trying to get this lovely little boy into the car.

It was not a nice thing for me to see – Carey began to growl at his owner immediately when the boot was opened and he was asked to jump in. When he refused to move she bent down to put her hand on his collar to help him and he flew at her. Yes she was scared of him, so of course she withdrew her hand. This is exactly what he wanted – he had won – why bother doing anything when a growl or snap means I don't have to.

So, fitting a comfy harness and long line we began again to ask of him a simple task. Getting into the car would mean an interesting life, more walks, more fun yet he hated the very thought. At times Jack Russells can be very stubborn and if for years they do not have to do what they are asked it can be hard to break through the barrier of determination versus strong will. Why would a dog do anything he is asked anyway? If there is not much positive outcome for him why bother?

Using a longer lead than normal I asked his owner to be more positive in her mind, that she was his guide and that he was getting in the car. There was an objection but using a longer lead it was possible to get out of the way of his attempts to snap, it meant Jill had more confidence and lifting him from the middle of his back with the comfy harness meaning his neck was not jerked he was in the car before he knew it and importantly immediate praise and treats were given.

I could see him thinking. He did not want to be grumpy. He was almost sorry.

We practised this several times, using different cars, mine and Jill's and then asking Doug and Jill's border terrier Millie to get in beside him, always following up with hugely positive prise and treats.

Jill and Carey, a miracle that he now gets in car without any objection at all. She is thrilled!!!! As am I.

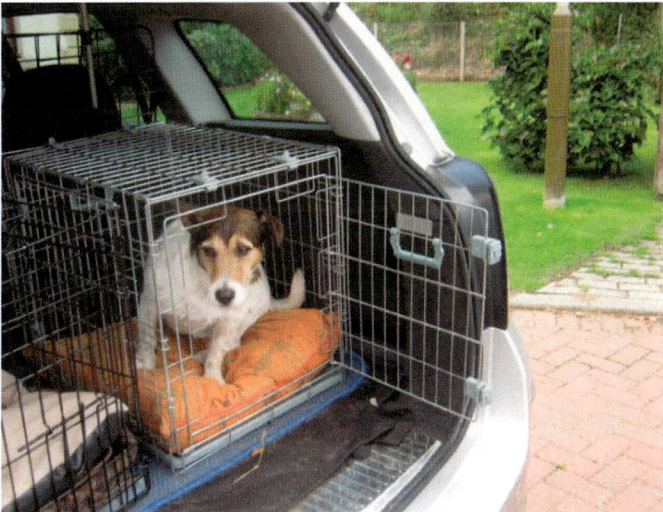

I hear things are going very nicely and that there has been much improvement, especially in that now Carey wolfs down all his meals without question.

I know that Carey was edgy and stressed out from being hungry and under nourished and was told that the change in him was almost immediate, which is wonderful news.

He had settled down a lot in a short space of time and it was becoming easier to get him to do as he was asked, with much less objection – and most of all Jill's Mum is a delighted and a re-established confident dog owner.

Kai

Marie with her daughter Claire and the handsome Kai.

It was while holding a charity dog wash in my grooming salon that I met a lovely lady called Marie.

Marie was with a friend, who had brought his Rottweiler in for a bath and she chatted to me briefly about her own dog having problems with his confidence because of an unfortunate accident. She was very upset because she had actually stopped trying to get him out for a walk and as the months were passing she was feeling more and more guilty and his behaviour at home was worrying. I was asked to go to her home the following week.

I was greeted at her front door by a highly excitable and very handsome young black Staffordshire terrier jumping up and running around the room and up on the furniture.

As we talked over the next hour or so Marie broke down in tears which is something I experience many times while I talk to people regarding their dogs' problems. It can be a highly emotive subject and it is common for me to hear people say how guilty they feel for not being able to help their own dogs. I have known people to spill out all sorts of reasons for why they feel things have gone wrong.

At times I feel like a counsellor and I know that the work I do with dogs is more often about solving a much deeper emotional issue with the owners and I am so grateful to be in a position to be part of their journey toward healing.

Nine months previously Kai had escaped from the front door, run out onto the road in front of the house and a car had hit him and dragged him a long distance up the road .A horrendous experience for any animal indeed any owner to witness.

The poor dog was hospitalised for a few days and luckily had no broken bones but was traumatised from his ordeal and once his wounds had healed he refused to go for a walk from the house, simply sitting down and refusing to go further and then running back into the house for safety.

The guilt which Marie was carrying about not being able to sort her dogs problems was an overwhelming emotion and too much for her to cope with. Not being able to walk her dog made her feel like a useless dog owner and she was desperate for help. Kai was barking at anything and everything that he could see from the lounge window and understandably was going a little stir crazy from lack of exercise and stimulation which is vital for a dog to be happy and balanced.

As usual after covering how to make changes within her home including moving Kais' bed from beside the window and making it less easy for him to be at the window all day, we talked about going for a walk.

A walk? Today?

Yes I said now we are going out.

I fitted a comfy harness and explained the long line.

I asked Marie and her daughter to walk out of the front door ahead of me and I followed holding Kai on an ordinary lead attached to his harness. I closed the front door behind me and because his owner was ahead of me Kai walked on. After two or three steps he suddenly realised what was happening and did an about turn but without hesitating I carried on and after he did a little spin beside me he realised I was not going to stop as his owner previously had, giving in to his fears, and remarkably he walked along beside me as though nothing had ever happened. I walked through the gate and turned left behind his owner. Kai followed with no hesitation and I asked myself what had been the problem here? I asked Marie how she was feeling. The answer was that Kai had never walked through the gate since his accident and she could not believe her eyes as to what she was seeing. The rest of the walk was a pleasure for both Kai and for Marie; I was relaxed and therefore so was Kai.

What had been happening previously was Kai had been nervous and tried to turn back to the house and so his owner who was understandably caught up in emotional thoughts about how he might be afraid, thought it was best to let him.

Using a harness he felt supported yet less forced into walking out and I was confident with him, showing him that there was no danger by my body language and in my thoughts.

If you are nervous or worried that something might happen when you take your dog for a walk, your dog will pick this up and be more likely to hesitate.

For both Kai and Marie the fear has never returned and I have regular positive updates regarding how much better life is for them. He has long walks every day which Marie absolutely loves and she tells me he is now a happy and relaxed boy and is no longer constantly barking at the window.

He now enjoys a varied diet of raw meats and bones and is a shining example of a well balanced, fit and healthy young dog.

He is no longer stressed.

Angela and family.

Angela and Poppy

"I have now stopped walking her and I feel so guilty, but I really do not know what else I can do. Can u help me?"

Having felt this exact feeling with my own dog Aloysious, I still remind myself how awful I felt and yet felt so stuck for a solution and did not know who to turn to. Thankfully for me and now many other dogs, together he and I devised the wonderful "Wish Come True" method of helping people with their dogs' problems.

Angela told me on the phone all about her little Shih Tzu Poppy, how she absolutely adores her, yet walking her had become a huge nightmare. Poppy pulled terribly which hurt Angela's shoulder and hands and when she saw another dog she simply went berserk, lunging and pulling and barking non stop. Angela was now filled with fear as to what may happen to her beloved dog if another dog attacked her and so she had decided she could no longer take her out.

This in itself was not the answer as it wracked Angela with guilt and she knew it was not the best solution for her little dog.

Angela booked me to go along that same evening.

When I arrived, I was met by a very small fluffy dog with a huge attitude. She simply would not stop barking at me. However as soon as I made any movement toward her she back away from me, yet continued her jumping up and barking non stop.

She was so noisy and excited I had to ask for her to be put away into another room so I could be heard. This is not something I would normally ask but when her owner eventually tried to stop her it made no difference. I felt it was better to begin helping her owners to learn reasons why she was so unruly and for that I needed peace.

After an hour or so explaining how to make small changes toward calming Poppy down and to take the responsibilities she felt she needed to carry away from her without her even knowing, we headed off out on a what her owner Angela now considered to be the dreaded walk.

So, fitting Poppy with a comfy harness and long line attached we ventured out along the street. I could quickly see how difficult things had been for Angela. Despite her size, Poppy was a very strong and determined little dog, almost hyperactive in her temperament and her constant relentless pulling really hurt Angela's hands and shoulder. I could see that a lot of work and effort would need to be put in with Poppy but also when I witness such behaviour it is always in my mind how much a processed diet can add to such levels of hyperactivity. I have proven it time and time again with my own dogs and my clients that when changing to a species appropriate diet dogs which are seemingly un-trainable begin to calm down and become balanced in their demeanour. It is never my place to insist or dictate to an owner to make the change but to inform through my observations and educate as to the reasons why their dog has behaviour issues and I wholeheartedly know how much the added ingredients, which are so often unknown in processed foods, can make an animal behave erratically.

We reached the field area at the end of the street and for the first time in all of her two years Poppy got to run freely at the end of her long twenty foot line. What a joy to behold, she didn't stop, she just didn't stop. This is what a dog needs, daily, every day come rain or shine in order to be balanced and healthy yet because her owner was afraid and also worn thin by her antics of pulling and barking when she sees another dog she had all but given up walking her completely. This is a very common occurrence and one which I am so grateful that I can help unravel for frustrated owners.

A well exercised dog is one with much less behaviour problems.

We let Poppy enjoy a long session of freedom and soon she was responding well to recall with Angela and I could see how happy they both now were.

Walking home Poppy was still pulling a lot but gradually I began to see improvement in the length of time she would stay at heel. I teach a technique which is not difficult to learn when dogs are very strong pullers, but it takes a lot of patience and consistency from owners.

When the dog reaches the end of its lead and you feel a tension between you, you simply stop. The dog will eventually turn and look at you and that split second you walk backwards and call him to you with open arms and much give huge praise and treats.

It is necessary to do this again and again in short training session in order for the dog to begin to realise he / she can only walk on a lead when there is no tension between you – i.e. a loose lead and yet be beside you – it can take a lot of patience and effort on your part but it is a very effective method of training.

Two weeks later I met up with Angela and Poppy again.

Angela told me that Poppy had improved hugely with her walking to heel and she no longer had a sore arm with her pulling as before but she wanted help to learn how to cope with her when she saw other dogs. Poppy would go berserk, lunging and barking at any dog she saw and Angela was very afraid as she could not control her antics.

Poppy lunging at another dog – all four feet off the ground.

We met at a busy park on a Sunday when it was more likely to see lots of dogs. Using two leads, one on Poppy's harness and one on her collar Angela felt more confident in controlling her when she went into her frenzy when she saw other dogs. Poppy would lift herself completely off the ground and bark constantly as though she was ferocious and at times almost trip up her owner. She was not aggressive however, she was simply frightened.

Angela facing the problem full on

Using two leads it was much easier to turn Poppy away from what frightened her and guide her in another direction. Doing this time and time again each time Poppy began to get excited it was soon obvious that her barking became less and soon ceased altogether.

I introduced one of my dogs Mollie, a lovely calm twelve year old cross spaniel/poodle to the equation.

I knew Mollie would not react to Poppy's tantrums and using her she would be teaching Poppy that there was no reason to feel fear. Sure enough when Poppy began to bark Mollie simply turned her head away and carried on walking alongside us. It was not long before I handed Mollies lead to Angela and all three were walking along calmly together.

Angela was able to walk Molly beside Poppy within minutes.

We had progress with other dogs too and within half an hour and Angela faced her fears confidently when I asked her to begin carefully walking closer to other approaching dogs whenever they appeared across the park. I am always vigilant when helping fearful owners and ready to assist if I see if a problem may arise.

Asking owners to tell me how they are feeling as we go through each process is a very important part of my training work and it is so rewarding to me to see an owner progress in confidence and be able to cope with their dogs in real every day situations when before they had simply given up trying.

Angela felt much more able to control Poppy's outbursts using two leads yet it was only a short space of time before they became less intense.

Angela walking past other dogs – Poppy here is much calmer.

I have no doubt that over time Poppy will calm down completely given the effort that Angela has put in with her.

The aim though here, is to keep up the training using both leads until there is a marked difference in how Poppy reacts before going back to using only one. Taking an extra lead out with you on a walk is not difficult to use when you feel there may be danger ahead can be a very good idea.

Annemarie and Patch

Annemarie and Patch

A phone call one Monday morning connected me with Annemarie and her lovely border collie dog Patch.

Her voice was shaky; the tones of desperation told me that help was needed quickly in order to help this owner as she was at her wits end as to what to do.

Patch was attacking other dogs and she could not control him so she had stopped taking him out anywhere she might see any other dogs and only at 6am or later in the evenings.

She had asked another behaviourist to help but felt there was little improvement in him or help to herself, in fact they had used bullying tactics to Patch in order to dominate him so as to get him to comform to what was expected.

I prefer to ask a dog to use his own mind to get over a problem when shown by someone who guides confidently. Trust is gained between owner and dog and behaviour improves naturally.

Patch had belonged to another family and only came to her at the age of three. He would growl at her if he did not like what she asked of him so she would back away from him. He was fed on dry processed food which was always available in a bowl on the floor. I noticed he was quite anxious even as he lay on the floor as we spoke, his ears constantly listening to external sounds and his eyes moving from side to side.

Fireworks would send him into a frenzy.

Patch walked close to heel, Annemarie had no pulling problems with him but because of his outbursts toward other dogs he was not allowed to run free very often. Using a harness and long line Patch thoroughly enjoyed using his nose to sniff along the ground and at trees and bushes as we walked along and when we reached a large open space he was allowed to run free at the end of the twenty foot line.

As can happen often when I am out on training sessions, we did not see many other dogs so I suggested a car trip to a further hopefully busier park.

In order to help someone get over their fears I have to help them face them.

I need to show them how they can control their dogs and help them when faced with the very thing that frightens them. Although Annemarie was fearful I had to see for myself how Patch reacted and therefore how to help Annemarie cope with him and to build up her confidence in the process.

When we reached the park we fitted a second lead to Patch on his collar and walked him closer to other dogs whenever we saw any. Keeping both leads as loose as possible so as not to instil any fear from his owner I asked Annemarie to walk closer to a dog and owner who were walking toward us on the other side of a wide path.

I knew Annemarie was not keen yet she faced her fear confidently and keeping herself between Patch and what he considered to be a threat they walked on. Patch did not react and keeping up with my encouragement Annemarie walked on past the other dog and round to her left in a circle back to me.

Considering that Annemarie had told me whenever she had previously seen another dog far away in the distance she would turn and head for home, this was a massive step forward for both of them.

Because Annemarie felt more in control of Patch and able to turn him away using two leads if he decided to lunge she felt confident enough to walk forward to show Patch there was nothing to fear.

I have since had reports from Annemarie saying that Patch still can get anxious at times but that she now does not and because of this she can guide him so much better before he goes into a full lunge.

Angela is one of the type of owners I do not see as often as I would like in that she always, always praised Patch without my prompting when he was biddable and relaxed so he knew what was good behaviour.

Timing is the key in such behaviour issues. Be one step ahead of your dog if you know he is susceptible to doing something be it barking or lunging at others. Remove them from the danger, the eye contact with what they are afraid of or threatened by and praise them as soon as they are relaxed, not while they are still tense.

I have no doubt that Patch will feel much less threatened by other dogs now that his guide is so much less fearful. At times it may not be possible to completely help a dog get over deep seated fears but to give them a much happier existence despite all odds by seeking help and support in how to go about coping with individual temperaments. Collies need to run, they need a job, they focus on objects intensely, it is what they were bred to do.

Patch enjoying more freedom at the end of a long line.

Patch would focus on a football in the park when kids were playing and his owner would worry that he would lunge at them. The answer was to carry her own ball and to use it to get his attention away from anything she did not want him to do, thus diffusing the situation.

I am so pleased that now a once frightened owner who was forced into not walking her dog can now walk him confidently and he has the daily stimulation he much needs.

Wish Flying Free

Recommended Reading

On Talking Terms With Dogs: Calming Signals by Turid Rugaas

Barking – The Sound of a Language by Turid Rugaas

The Canine Thyroid Epidemic by Dr Jean Dodds

The Science Behind Canine Raw Feeding by H B Turner

The Science Behind Canine Behaviour by H B Turner

Useful Links

www.annahp.co.uk

www.canine-health-concern.org.uk

www.dog-games.co.uk

www.imapuppymummy.com

www.tilleyfarm.co.uk

www.yellowdoguk.co.uk

'Wish Come True' and 'The ARK' can be found on facebook.

4131703R00053

Printed in Great Britain
by Amazon.co.uk, Ltd.,
Marston Gate.